CURRENCY CONTROL

CURRENCY CONTROL

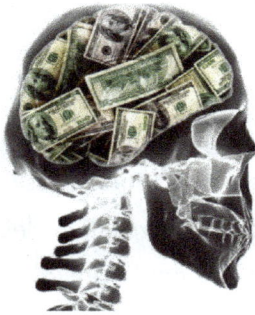

A MONEY MANAGEMENT GUIDE TO WEALTH
AND FINANCIAL FREEDOM

JAMALL LYNCH

Print ISBN:9798218925307
eBook ISBN:9798218925314

DEDICATED TO ALL THE
INDIVIDUALS WHO
ASPIRE TO BECOME
FINANCIALLY FREE

Contents

Introduction   10

1. The 4 Types of Money   14

2. Financial Education   30

3. Identifying Your Intelligence   42

4. Power of the Subconscious Mind   54

5. Discipline Vs. Motivation   68

6. Cash Is King And Credit Is Queen   80

7. Channeling Emotions   96

8. The Ultimate Sacrifice   108

9. Business and Investing   118

10. Transformation Requires Isolation   132

INTRODUCTION

The United States of America is undeniably known as the richest country in the world. So why is it that only 1% of Americans are truly wealthy? And why do 70% of people live paycheck to paycheck? The answer to both lies in a lack of financial literacy.

This is a place where opportunities are boundless and money is plentiful, yet the majority of its people still struggle to hold onto it—or perhaps, the people themselves struggle to attract money.

Currency Control is a straightforward and easy-to-understand guide that explores the connection between human behavior and personal finances. This book is far from your typical finance read. It dives deep into how emotions significantly influence how we handle money. With the various stories and ideas shared in each chapter, I promise you'll begin adopting better money habits right away.

Having worked for a former Fortune 500 company and as an entrepreneur, I was able to apply and uphold all the principles from this book. In fact, it has helped me maintain my business through cautious spending and taught me the essentials of mastering the financial game.

Currency Control will certainly boost your financial intelligence, so don't hesitate to dive into its pages. Start reading today if you truly want to transform your financial future forever.

1.
THE 4 TYPES
OF
MONEY

"MONEY DOESN'T FOLLOW FAIRNESS; IT FOLLOWS POWER, AND POWER IS NEVER GRANTED, IT'S SEIZED"

What does it truly mean to be successful? Depending on who you ask, success can have two very different meanings. For a young, ambitious person just starting out on their journey, success might signify one thing.

However, someone more experienced is likely to have a completely different understanding of what success entails.

In today's world, where social media plays a powerful role, success is often seen in terms of how much money you make and the material possessions you own. I'm not here to criticize prominent figures in professional sports or the entertainment industry, but the truth is that those with a large voice and platform are typically the ones who shape the opinions of the majority.

Let's be honest, if your favorite athlete or musician keeps showing off their wealth on social media for long enough, eventually those who watch closely will start to believe that success is only about making an enormous amount of money or owning the most expensive car and house. I admit that without money, it would be tough for anyone to sustain a stable lifestyle. I know bills must be paid, and food must be provided for you and your family. I also understand why many of us link money with success.

Since the beginning of time, acquiring money has always played a role in driving progress forward. What I have learned through my studies, research, and experience, however, is that success means something entirely different. I encountered this idea after facing failures and confronting challenges head-on. My conclusion is that success is the ongoing pursuit of a meaningful goal. In other words, if a person has a clear objective with a plan of action and is actively working toward it, they are already successful.

As unusual as it may sound, the late great Earl Nightingale, known for his motivational spirit, was a popular radio speaker and author. His belief was that success doesn't come from making money; instead, making money follows success. Earl taught that to consider yourself successful, you first have to be diligently working on your goals, and money will come as a result. This money is essentially a byproduct of the law of attraction. Earl called this idea "The Strangest Secret in the World."

What truly defines success is who you become during the journey. For years, the false idea of success has been focused on how much money a person has and the possessions they own, but the truth is, success has little to do with either.

Why is discussing success so important?

When we truly understand what success means, we become better at managing money.

If money is the only reason someone pursues something, they're more likely to quit when things get tough. But if your purpose is bigger than just earning an income, you'll be able to handle life's challenges more effectively.

To control money, we first need to truly understand what money is. Money is a vector that carries value. For example, imagine Louis Vuitton, the famous luxury brand, just launched a new style of women's tote bag priced at $3,000. You spend $3,000 to buy the bag. Where does the value lie, in the $3,000 or the bag itself? This question depends on how an individual views value. In theory, money exists to represent value, so essentially the product and the brand name hold greater value because of perception. If Louis Vuitton suddenly went bankrupt and started discounting all its products, they probably wouldn't hold the same value because of the shift in perception.

It's odd how many people associate value with high price tags, yet the most valuable things in life, from a technological point of view, were given to us for free. Our minds, bodies, spirits, and the love of family are things many of us overlook and undervalue compared to material goods.

To truly master the money game, we have to learn about and understand the four types of money in our current economy. Once we are knowledgeable about all forms of money, we can use them wisely to build lasting wealth.

FIAT MONEY

Fiat currency is what most of us recognize as money. This refers to the paper bills we're all familiar with. These well-known notes come in seven denominations: $100, $50, $20, $10, $5, $2, and $1. Fiat currency is issued by a government and is not backed by a physical commodity like gold. Its value comes from the government declaring it legal tender.

Essentially, its worth depends on the trust people place in the government that issues it and the stability of its economy.

It's quite fascinating that today's fiat money isn't tied to any physical commodity, but before

1971, it was backed by gold. That's right—back then, you could take those dollar bills we all appreciate to a bank and exchange them for gold. Those were the good old days. However, in 1971, a major shift took place in the monetary system. President Richard Nixon decided to remove the U.S. dollar from the gold standard. The reason behind this move was to control inflation and avoid an economic crisis after the Great Depression. Back then, the U.S. held more gold than any other country, and its dollar was considered the world's reserve currency. This meant that the U.S. dollar circulated widely in foreign nations, and those countries had the option to convert their dollars into gold. When Nixon realized the risk of a bank run—with many nations potentially trying to exchange their U.S. dollars for gold amid financial panic—he acted to protect U.S. wealth. He understood that there were more dollars held overseas than gold reserves to back them.

To prevent the U.S. from going bankrupt, he made what I like to call the ultimate chess move.

This allowed the U.S. to print more money, maintaining the appearance of value even though the currency was no longer tied to a physical asset. By that time, the psychological impact was already set: the world still regarded the dollar as valuable, and it remained the official currency for trade in many countries. Needless to say, the U.S. dollar continues to be the world's reserve currency, and it doesn't seem like any other currency will replace it anytime soon. Despite the rise of cryptocurrencies and discussions about a possible new currency from the BRICS nations (Brazil, Russia, India, China, and South Africa), many so-called experts predict these could become dominant reserve currencies—though this is purely speculative.

It's safe to say that the Gold Standard is why so many of us link paper money with success. The irony is that the only reason fiat currency is seen as valuable is that it once could be converted into gold. After Nixon ended that link, the dollar essentially became without real worth, yet in the eyes of the public, it still holds value, even without intrinsic worth.

COMMODITY MONEY

Commodity currency is a type of money made from a physical item that has inherent value. This means the item itself is valuable naturally. Examples include gold, silver, oil, and cattle. Unlike fiat currency, the material it's made from is valuable on its own.

In earlier times, before paper and coin money existed, people traded using the barter system— exchanging goods and services directly. For example, if you wanted cattle, you might have asked a neighbor if they were willing to trade their cattle for your oil, assuming they needed it. Or if you had silver and required construction work on your land, you could have traded your silver with someone skilled in building, provided they accepted it.

Over time, we grew wiser and more sophisticated in how we traded. Eventually, it must have become incredibly frustrating to carry around all those physical goods just to buy daily essentials, which is likely why we switched to using fiat currency.

A few years ago, I had the chance to travel to Los Angeles, California, to attend a trade show for my business. It was surprising to discover that a large community in California still uses the barter system for exchanging goods and services. Many countries around the world also continue to rely on this method of trade. This highlights just how varied money truly is.

COMMERCIAL BANK MONEY

Commercial bank money refers to the portion of the money supply generated when banks issue loans and create deposits. A simple way to describe commercial bank money is as book money—money that represents debt claims. When a bank approves a loan, it creates a new deposit in the borrower's account, instantly adding new money to the economy.

Examples include checking and savings account balances, mortgages, auto loans, credit card balances, and checks.

Another interesting fact is that our current banking system creates money through the fractional reserve banking system. This means that banks use deposited money to generate multiple times that amount. For example, if you deposit $1,000, the bank can lend out $10,000 using this system. This is how money expands in today's banking environment.

Have you ever wondered why banks pay so little interest on your deposits? It's because they know most savers don't invest their money themselves. Instead, the banks invest your funds for you across various markets.

Believe it or not, this practice is completely legal. When you deposit money, the bank legally owns it under federal law, even though they are obligated to return your funds upon request.

The only time it's difficult to withdraw your money is if the bank is about to collapse or if your deposits exceed the $250,000 federal insurance limit. History has shown numerous cases where banks became over leveraged during financial crises. In such moments, panic can lead to a bank run, where customers rush to withdraw funds unaware that the bank lacks enough cash to pay everyone back, causing the bank to fail. Recent examples include the collapses of Silicon Valley Bank and Signature Bank in 2023.

FIDUCIARY MONEY

Fiduciary money is a type of currency that derives its value from the trust and confidence that the issuer will exchange it for a commodity or fiat money later on. This money isn't government-issued legal tender. Examples include banknotes, checks, and electronic credits, which people accept because they trust the promise of payment.

The four types of currency collectively keep our economy moving. The more you learn about each, the better you can understand their roles and make smart financial decisions. I find it quite ironic that financial literacy is rarely emphasized in our education system. Even more surprising is how little money is talked about in most households. I say this confidently after reading a recent Bankrate report revealing that 59% of Americans couldn't cover a $1,000 emergency expense.

A different survey done by Forbes found that over one in four Americans, approximately 28%, had savings under $1000. How is it that the richest country in the world and the biggest consumer globally has such a large portion of its population living in poverty? I could likely provide an answer, but for now, you'll have to decide for yourself.

CHAPTER HIGHLIGHTS

1. Grasping the different types and roles of money will help you become more financially knowledgeable.

2. Success is truly defined as the ongoing pursuit of a meaningful goal. Anyone with a clear objective who is actively striving toward it is already successful.

3. Money acts as a vehicle that carries and conveys value.

2.
FINANCIAL
EDUCATION

"FINANCIAL INDEPENDENCE MEANS HAVING THE CAPACITY TO SUPPORT YOURSELF USING THE INCOME GENERATED FROM YOUR OWN ASSETS"

Junior Bridgeman's story ranks among the most inspiring I've ever encountered. Before his unexpected passing, he was recognized as one of the wealthiest African Americans, with a net worth reported to exceed $6 billion. He was also cited as one of the richest former athletes globally.

Born in Indiana, Junior played college basketball at the University of Louisville before being drafted in the first round of the 1975 NBA draft. Anyone familiar with professional basketball knows how exceptional a player must be to be drafted, especially by a legendary team like the Los Angeles Lakers—a clear testament to his talent. Standing 6 feet 5 inches tall, Bridgeman played as a small forward/shooting guard. He later played for the Los Angeles Clippers and the

Milwaukee Bucks, finishing his career with averages of 13.6 points, 3.5 rebounds, and 2.4 assists per game. While these numbers don't match the heights of a Michael Jordan, they are still respectable.

During his NBA career, his salary never exceeded $350,000, which, although decent, was modest compared to some of his superstar peers. At the time, Bridgeman was one of those players who didn't often make the headlines.

Despite his professional basketball career, Bridgeman worked at the Wendy's fast-food chain during the off-season. He dedicated himself to learning the business's workings, aiming to invest in the franchise after retiring from basketball. Junior understood early on that his NBA salary alone wouldn't carry him far, especially given the many stories of athletes who went broke after retirement.

He crafted a plan, set a strategy, and turned that vision into reality. Eventually, he owned 450 fast-food restaurants, including over 160 Wendy's and 120 Chili's locations. Bridgeman also founded a Coca-Cola bottling company to distribute beverage brands. In 2016, Forbes ranked him as the fourth wealthiest retired athlete in the world, trailing only Michael Jordan, David Beckham, and Arnold Palmer.

In 2020, he acquired Ebony and Jet magazines after they both filed for bankruptcy. Not bad for a kid from East Chicago, Indiana.

So, how did Junior Bridgeman outpace his peers financially? The answer lies in financial intelligence. Bridgeman used his NBA earnings strategically to build long-term wealth for himself and his family. He wasn't afraid to take a few steps back to make larger strides forward. He raised his financial IQ by focusing on the long game—a game many avoid. With so much emphasis on overnight success stories, it's no surprise people fall for get-rich-quick schemes. But the truth is, genuine wealth is seldom amassed overnight. It requires years of effort, patience, and a bit of luck. Sure, some get rich quickly by chance, but just as fast as it's gained, it can be lost.

To maintain wealth, one must embrace financial education, and only then do we realize that the super wealthy don't work for money. I'll explore this topic further later in the chapter.

To become financially literate, we must first understand what financial education means. The best definition I've found is this: financial education is the knowledge and understanding of how money is earned, spent, and saved, along with the skills needed to manage financial resources and make informed decisions. In short, financial education is your ability to control cash flow. Are you someone who spends impulsively, or do you save with the intention of building wealth? No matter what your spending habits are, it's essential to understand that most people's financial choices are shaped by their behavior and emotions. Factors like stress, anxiety, the need for social status, upbringing, and past experiences all influence how someone handles money.

To manage your finances well, a good approach is to use your emotions thoughtfully rather than letting them control your decisions, which requires a lot of self-discipline. I recall reading a well-known book some time ago called "The Richest Man In Babylon" by George S. Clason. This book teaches personal finance lessons through ancient Babylonian parables. Its key message is powerful: wealth grows through disciplined habits. What I learned from it is to save at least 10% of every dollar you earn, keep your expenses low, and make every dollar work for you by investing wisely. These three principles have stayed with me and truly suit my current lifestyle. Another valuable lesson from the book is to plan ahead for future income because, as you age, you want to protect yourself from financial difficulties. Also, always work on enhancing your earning ability by expanding your skills and knowledge.

There are three major traits that reduce a person's chances of success: arrogance, laziness, and ignorance.

"The rich don't work for money" is the opening lesson in Robert Kiyosaki's widely praised book "Rich Dad Poor Dad," often regarded as the top finance book ever. I admit, when I first read that chapter, I was stunned. I remember thinking to myself, what on earth is this guy saying? If rich people don't work for money, then what are they working for, I wondered. Looking back, I realize how arrogantly clueless I sounded, and I now appreciate the deeper insights the book offers. As I continued reading, I came to understand that Robert meant the wealthy work for assets that generate money for them. These assets include things like rental properties that provide steady cash flow every month, whether you work or not, or investments in businesses where you're not actively involved but still receive an annual return. Depending on whom you ask, an asset is defined as something that puts money into your pocket, while a liability takes money out.

"Rich Dad Poor Dad" challenged traditional views on personal finance and sparked debate, especially after Robert appeared on Oprah to promote the book. When he said that a personal residence (which isn't an investment property) isn't truly an asset, financial experts exploded. Most people think a house is an asset, but according to Robert and many financial pros, if you have to use your earned money to cover its expenses, then your home is actually a liability. Experts are divided on this idea, but if you pause to really think about it, it makes sense, even if it's a bit convoluted. After fully absorbing this lesson, I immediately wanted to learn how to turn costly liabilities—things I had wasted money on—into cash-generating assets. I've realized that money is a subject that requires constant study.

You can never get too comfortable with your financial education because it's such a wide topic. The best way to understand your money habits is to commit yourself to lifelong learning. Imagine if heart surgeons stopped studying their craft or lawyers stopped updating their knowledge of new laws—they'd lose their edge and wouldn't perform well. The same applies to financial education. No affluent individual who has accumulated significant wealth has ever stopped educating themselves about finances.

CHAPTER HIGHLIGHTS

1. Financial education means understanding how money is earned, used, and saved, along with having the skills to manage financial resources to make informed choices.

2. Set aside 10% of every dollar you make and invest it carefully.

3. Control your expenses and keep track of your money coming in and going out.

3.

IDENTIFYING
YOUR
INTELLIGENCE

"INTELLIGENCE INCREASES OUR AWARENESS WHILE ALSO INTENSIFYING OUR SENSITIVITIES TO PAIN AND FLAWS"

Has anyone ever asked you what your purpose in life is? If you don't have an answer, that's completely fine. It can take years to discover your life's true purpose. The first time I was asked that question, I was genuinely stuck. I spent years pondering it. It puzzled me so much that I couldn't grasp how I had been living without knowing my purpose all that time. That's when I realized I needed to put a lot of effort into understanding myself to uncover what my purpose might be. It took many years before I finally found it.

One important thing to mention is that life didn't feel fulfilling back then, and I wasn't proud of where I was. Sure, I had a job and a career earning decent money, but something just didn't feel right.

Studies have shown that the number one trait that highlights your uniqueness as an individual is your ability to question. I began asking myself open-ended questions instead of making vague statements. For instance, I would ask myself, "How can I discover my life's purpose?" instead of saying, "It's so hard to find my life's purpose." When you ask open-ended questions, you activate the frontal lobe, the part of the brain responsible for thinking, memory, and behavior. Asking questions forces you to think, which encourages your brain to form logic and create action plans. If you ask yourself enough open-ended questions, you will definitely notice a change. I should add that living without a purpose is like having no direction in life. This is important because I truly believe that when someone has no meaning or purpose, managing finances can become a nightmare.

Throughout history, some of the wealthiest people in the world have operated based on their life's mission. For example, Bill Gates is focusing on revolutionizing agriculture after building billions in net worth from Microsoft. Similarly, Elon Musk is aiming to create a self-sustaining human civilization on Mars after quadrupling his fortune through Tesla. These men have made more money than most could dream of—enough to support the average American for ten lifetimes—yet they remain driven by purpose. At this point, it's clear that Bill and Elon are using their wealth to fund their missions and fulfill their life's purposes.

Don't confuse passion with purpose.

Passion fuels your emotional drive to do what you love, while purpose involves contributing to others and serving something greater than yourself. You might be wondering how to find your own purpose. I won't tell you what you should do, but I can certainly share what helped me discover mine.

First, I assessed my skills. Then I started exploring books on personal development and self-help, where I came across the concept of the seven intelligences. A developmental psychologist and professor of cognition and education at Harvard's graduate school, Howard Gardner proposed that intelligence isn't just one thing but seven different kinds.

He believed that people have varied intelligences and learn or process information in different ways.

Ironically, most of us only associate intelligence with academic success, which Gardner argued isn't always accurate. Let's take a closer look at each intelligence and dig deeper.

VERBAL-LINGUISTIC

These individuals excel academically. They are your top students, often naturally gifted with verbal-linguistic intelligence. They are skilled readers and writers. People with this intelligence commonly pursue careers as Authors or Lawyers.

LOGICAL-MATHEMATICAL

Those who enjoy working with numbers and solving math problems tend to have this intelligence. They can solve equations faster than a calculator thanks to this talent. Many go on to earn advanced degrees and become teachers, professors, or researchers. They might work for universities, corporations, or government agencies. Students who perform well in math often gravitate toward fields like accounting, computer programming, or engineering.

BODY-KINESTHETIC

Athletes often possess this kind of intelligence. Those who excel usually become professional athletes or dancers. They also tend to pursue careers in health or recreational fields.

SPATIAL

People with spatial intelligence often have a strong passion for the arts. They frequently attend art schools aiming to become successful artists. Those with this intelligence often become architects, designers, graphic artists, or website developers.

MUSICAL

Musically intelligent individuals dream of fame in the music world. They quickly pick up instruments and develop familiarity. Even listening to music boosts their intelligence and inspires them to create. Those with this gift commonly seek careers in the music industry.

INTERPERSONAL

This intelligence is vital for professions involving communication, such as Preachers, Politicians, and Sales experts. If you naturally have strong interpersonal skills, it means you're good at meeting new people, building relationships, and making friends.

INTRAPERSONAL

While interpersonal intelligence is about interacting with others, intrapersonal intelligence is your inner communication—how well you understand and control your own thoughts. People with this intelligence manage their emotions effectively. Intrapersonal intelligence, closely linked to emotional intelligence, will be explored further in a later chapter. Those who have it often become Entrepreneurs. This intelligence, often seen as key to success, gives entrepreneurs a major edge in business. It empowers you to face challenges others avoid and makes you highly aware of your feelings and motivations.

Now that you're familiar with the seven intelligences, take some time to reflect on each one to better understand where you fit in. Since people can possess more than one intelligence, when I discovered mine, I had a revealing dream that instantly clarified my life's purpose. This insight was the missing piece I had been searching for. I don't expect you to use this as a blueprint, since everyone's path is different.

But perhaps this knowledge will help you move closer to discovering your own purpose, if you haven't already.

My conclusion is that purpose is connected to money management. Think about it: imagine you're broke with a negative bank balance, and suddenly you inherit $1 million. If you had no direction or guidance before receiving that money, what would happen after? You might go on a shopping spree, give generously to friends and family, and without financial intelligence, find yourself broke again before long.

This is a story that happens over and over. Whether it's someone who wins the lottery or a professional athlete who goes bankrupt five years after signing a $50 million contract, the outcome is often the same. When a person clearly defines their life's purpose, they become the true masters of their finances, opening doors they once thought were out of reach.

CHAPTER HIGHLIGHTS

1. Discover your life's purpose to lead a more meaningful life.

2. Identify your different intelligences and focus on developing each one step by step.

3. Your mission will present numerous opportunities.

4.

POWER
OF THE
SUBCONSCIOUS
MIND

"IF YOU CHANGE THE WAY
YOU LOOK AT THINGS,
THE THINGS YOU LOOK AT
CHANGE"

In 2019, I had been working for a former Fortune 500 company for about 15 years. I climbed the ranks through hard work and was rewarded with a significant management position and a respectable salary. However, by the end of that year, I was completely burned out—both physically and mentally. I knew that taking on a leadership role came with increased responsibilities and greater challenges, and I welcomed that journey, but deep down, I sensed something was missing. On top of that, I felt trapped by the corporate system, where the routine seemed to be work hard, save for retirement, and then pass away. Honestly, this is the pattern many of us follow. I believed there had to be more to life than what I had been taught. At that moment, I realized I needed to make a change but wasn't sure where or how to begin.

Fast forward to January 2020, I made a firm decision to improve my life. I started by reading articles and books, and listening to numerous podcasts about self-help, wealth, and financial education. Although I kept my job, I dedicated time to studying and planning my next move. I was driven and determined to find another path so I could eventually leave my job. After so many years with the company, I recognized I had hit a ceiling and didn't see further advancement ahead.

Then, one evening in March 2020, something happened that changed my life's direction—seemingly at the perfect time. Covid-19 was declared a highly contagious and deadly virus, leading to shutdowns across the U.S. and much of the world. In my hometown of New York City, everyone was required to stay indoors. I was furloughed from my job for three and a half months. I remained optimistic and believed this was an opportunity I needed to seize. A long break and a chance to reset my life was exactly what I wanted.

Please don't misunderstand me—I realize many people lost their lives and loved ones during this time, including myself. It was undeniably a difficult period for the world, and I respect that deeply. But I've learned that in tough times, it's essential to find optimism, which is exactly what I tried to do. I used my time away from work to reset, recharge, and reinvent my life. During that period, I discovered that my next path was entre-preneurship, a choice that aligned with my true purpose. A year later, I quit my job and moved on to a more fulfilling career.

This story matters because many of us carry mental programs that hold us back, often with-out realizing it. These programs might come from childhood, family influences, or educators. What if I told you that your life is a reflection of these mental programs because 95% of what you do stems from your subconscious mind? I'm here to say that it's possible to align your subconscious programs with the hopes, desires, and goals you hold in your conscious mind. Your brain is ready to absorb new information twice a day, which is the perfect opportunity to reprogram your subconscious. That's exactly what I did during those three and a half months off work, and it was the crucial factor in my transformation.

To clarify, the conscious and subconscious minds are separate entities. The conscious mind can learn through reading self-help books, attending lectures, or watching movies. It acquires information in many ways, but strangely, it isn't directly connected to the subconscious mind. Just because the conscious mind learns something doesn't mean the subconscious mind absorbs it too. The conscious mind learns creatively, while the subconscious mind learns habitually.

There are two ways to implant programs into the subconscious mind. The first method happens during the first seven years of life when we absorb information into the subconscious. At this stage, the subconscious mind operates at a theta vibrational frequency, which is essentially hypnosis. This means information can be directly downloaded into the subconscious when the mind enters a hypnotic state. Now, you might be thinking, "I'm not seven years old, nor do I have a child's brain," which brings me to the second method. Twice daily, your brain enters a phase of theta vibrational activity, meaning it's primed to absorb information through hypnosis. These moments occur just before going to sleep and immediately upon waking up. These times are ideal for playing mental recordings aimed at reprogramming your subconscious. This is why experts say the best time to teach children lasting programs is during their first seven years— they're continually in a hypnotic state then. This is where the phrase "children are like sponges" comes from. After age seven, the most effective way to return to a hypnotic state is within the first hour after waking and the hour before sleeping.

If you're dealing with financial troubles, addictions, or harmful habits, a useful approach is to play recordings of your desired outcomes. For example, if you want to become a millionaire, you might listen to recordings from platforms like YouTube focused on that goal. I challenge you to listen to such a program daily for 30 consecutive days. I assure you, if you remain consistent for 30 days, you will reprogram your mind so that it begins to work toward your goals almost automatically. Continuing beyond 30 days will bring even more transformation— you'll become unrecognizable. However, I must clarify this isn't some magic trick; it takes discipline and action. In my opinion, if you want to change your life's direction, this is hands down the best place to start. It's a hidden secret many wealthy people use to build their empires and a strategy athletes employ to excel at their sports. In fact, it's said that Mike Tyson, the former world heavyweight boxing champion, used to hire a hypnotist before major fights as part of his training, listening to programs that reinforced his goal of being the champ.

Another effective way to enter the theta state is through self-hypnosis, which I've personally tried and can confirm works well if done correctly. Since the subconscious learns and downloads information through repetition, chanting affirmations throughout the day can help you become a better version of yourself. Repeat these affirmations during your commute, in the shower, or between activities. You can also use recordings for this purpose.

Even if you're not fully focused on the recording, your subconscious is still absorbing the information. The subconscious mind is truly remarkable.

According to a study by Investopedia, 70% of Americans live paycheck to paycheck, a 4% increase from the previous year. This highlights one important truth: most Americans are struggling financially. We constantly hear about people facing difficulties due to higher living costs, inflation, and economic uncertainty. I agree that all these factors play a role, but there's one aspect many reports miss: the large number of Americans living paycheck to paycheck stems from ingrained programs embedded in the subconscious.

It's well-known that many of us had parents who lacked financial literacy and passed down their money beliefs. And if your parents rarely talked about money when you were a child, you likely inherited their views on finances. Without learning proper saving or investing habits as a teenager, it becomes very difficult to shift that mindset later in life. To be clear, it is possible to change, but it requires time and determination to rewire the subconscious after years of unhelpful money habits.

Many of us have been conditioned to improve our lifestyle only when we earn more or get a raise. For example, you might get a promotion and see a $10,000 boost in your salary—going from $70,000 to $80,000 a year. Before you realize it, you're putting down a payment on a new car, funding a family trip, or doubling how often you dine out each week.

Americans often feel the pressure to keep up with the Joneses, which traps them in a cycle of overspending. Instead of managing money wisely when income increases, we tend to spend more, continuing the cycle of financial struggle. Much of our financial trouble comes from what we're taught or who influences us. I've met many people earning six figures who struggle with money, while others making just above the poverty line are savvy and financially secure. Most of us don't live paycheck to paycheck due to a lack of money; it's because of behavior patterns shaped by past money programming.

CHAPTER HIGHLIGHTS

1. The subconscious mind serves as the key to unlocking wealth and abundance.

2. Affirmations are essential in personal growth.

3. Clearly define and focus on your goals when aiming to manifest them.

5.

DISCIPLINE VS. MOTIVATION

"I'D PREFER TO ENDURE
THE DISCOMFORT OF
DISCIPLINE THAN
TO FACE THE
PAIN OF REGRET"

Rapper, producer, and business mogul 50 Cent launched his music career in 1996, aiming to become a major superstar. By 1999, he had recorded his first official single, "How To Rob," intended for his original debut album "Power Of The Dollar." Although the album was ultimately shelved, the song received radio play and was featured on the soundtrack of the 1999 film "In Too Deep." The track stirred controversy as 50 Cent humorously took shots at rival rappers and other entertainers. His efforts seemed to pay off when high-profile artists like Jay-Z responded with diss tracks targeting him. For 50 Cent, this recognition was a significant honor and achievement, as having one of the biggest rappers reference him had been part of his marketing plan all along.

Just as 50 Cent began generating a buzz in the music industry, tragedy struck. He was shot multiple times, and it seemed his music career might be over. Yet, the unexpected occurred.

Over the next few years, 50 Cent recovered from his injuries and redirected all his energy and focus back into his music. In 2002, he flooded the underground hip-hop scene with numerous songs and mixtapes, which eventually caught the attention of Eminem and Dr. Dre, two major figures in the music world at that time. He signed a record deal with these rap giants, who helped produce his highly anticipated debut album, "Get Rich Or Die Tryin." The album became the biggest hip-hop debut ever released, selling over 872,000 copies in its first week. In 2003, 50 Cent rose to global superstardom, and his album achieved 10X platinum status—an achievement most musicians dream of but few reach.

50 Cent's story embodies discipline and motivation. He had a clear plan to become the

biggest artist and actively worked toward that goal. Despite facing setbacks, he never let them derail him, even while recovering from serious injuries. Something deep within him drove him to keep pushing toward his dream.

From his journey, we can learn that action sparks motivation, motivation breeds discipline, discipline leads to success, and success brings freedom. One key reason many struggle financially is due to a lack of discipline.

In his book "Atomic Habits," author James Clear offers a blueprint for developing good habits and breaking bad ones through small, gradual changes. The central idea is that tiny habits, when compounded over time, yield remarkable results. The book also explains fundamental principles of habit formation, helping readers achieve more by focusing on less. To manage your finances effectively, you must first break harmful habits and establish positive ones. If you want true financial freedom, you need to treat your money habits seriously.

A good place to start is by reviewing your monthly spending through your bank and credit card statements, tracking how much money is coming in versus what's going out. It's straightforward: if more money is leaving your account than entering it, it's a clear sign to change your spending habits. Begin by cutting unnecessary expenses, even something as minor as an app subscription. Another helpful habit is redirecting money spent on needless costs toward something that benefits you and your family longterm. For instance, if you discover $50 a month is automatically deducted for services you don't use, consider putting that $50 toward a $500,000 term life insurance policy. Alternatively, you might contribute that money to your retirement fund, like a 401K.

The key idea is that for every bad habit, you should replace it with a good one, and over time, this will create a positive compounded effect. I believe that success in any area of life depends on about 80% discipline and 20% motivation. This is because motivation is relatively easy to spark.

You can watch an inspiring video and feel highly motivated that same day. However, the excitement from that video can easily fade by the next day. What motivates you today may not inspire you tomorrow, since motivation has a limited shelf life. When motivation dwindles, discipline is what keeps the flame alive to reach your goals; without it, your dreams won't happen.

Every time you choose discipline over impulse, your inner strength grows stronger. Discipline means taking control and deliberately guiding your actions towards your goals. It's not about punishing yourself, but about doing things you may not want to because you understand they're best for your future. Discipline is why someone on a weight loss journey might shed 50 pounds in five months or why a new employee rises to manager within their first year. It's about building good habits and consistently sticking to them regardless of the situation.

Life is filled with noise and distractions, so it's unsurprising that attention spans keep shrinking. Part of this is due to conformity. We live in a world where being average is perfectly acceptable, and most people settle into mediocrity rather than standing out. I admit I'm not a fan of multitasking. Although I can multitask, I find it counterproductive. From my experience, multitasking leads to burnout and stagnation. How can you fully complete tasks if you're trying to do too many at once?

The word FOCUS is an acronym for Follow One Course Until Successful. I often use acronyms to help with ongoing learning, and this one really resonated with me. It works very well; whenever life feels overwhelming, I remind myself of this to regain my direction. I strongly believe that doing one thing at a time makes you more efficient and productive.

If you want to be more disciplined with your money, start by creating a budget and stick to it as closely as possible. Then, set clear, specific financial goals that will make a strong impact on your life. Next, automate your savings to build long-term wealth. After that, monitor your spending to see where your money goes. Fifth, even though it can be hard, pay off any existing debts as quickly as you can, even if it means paying more than the minimum. Sixth, establish an emergency fund to cover six months to a year of living expenses in case something unexpected happens. Lastly, and most importantly, reduce impulse buying and resist temptation. This will help keep you on track with your financial plan.

CHAPTER HIGHLIGHTS

1. Motivation tends to be short-lived.

2. What really shapes your character is discipline.

3. Each person is shaped by their every-day routines. Swap out each bad habit for a good one, and over time, it will create a positive, lasting impact.

6.
CASH IS KING AND CREDIT IS QUEEN

"TRUE WEALTH
IS COUNTED
IN MOMENTS,
NOT IN MONEY"

The largest financial crime ever committed in U.S. history, and possibly worldwide, was orchestrated by a man who once served as chairman of NASDAQ's board of directors.

His name was Bernard "Bernie" Madoff.

Before becoming a fraudster and con artist, Madoff ran a legitimate company. That firm played a crucial role in helping to computerize the over-the-counter stock market and contributed to the creation of the NASDAQ (National Association of Securities Dealers Automated Quotations) stock market. Anyone familiar with stock trading knows that NASDAQ is the second largest stock exchange globally by market capitalization. Unlike the NYSE (New York Stock Exchange), it has no physical trading floor;

instead, all trades are carried out via a computerized network and automated systems. One could say that the speed and efficiency of trades for some of the world's largest companies can be partly credited to Bernie Madoff. So, why would such a brilliant man turn to crime? Hold that thought; I'll come back to that question later.

First, let me explain how the scheme worked. Alongside his legitimate business, Madoff ran an advisory firm that wasn't properly registered, which allowed him to deceive investors out of an estimated $65 billion. This business operated with a sophisticated strategy involving blue-chip stocks and options to produce steady, high returns for clients. The advisory operation would use money from new investors to pay off earlier investors. In truth, no real trading was taking place. To be fair, this fraudulent activity didn't begin until the 1990s. Initially, Madoff did run a genuine business, but he somehow switched gears once he saw how easy it was to manipulate his clients. Madoff was so thorough in his deception that he built a strong reputation as the man who could consistently deliver 18%-20% returns—a dream for any investor.

Bernie Madoff expanded his scheme by entering circles of wealthy individuals, aiming to draw them into his Ponzi scheme. It was truly diabolical how he leveraged the strong reputation he had built on Wall Street to convince some of these investors. He did so subtly, not aggressively. Most investors came in through word of mouth. Occasionally, when a potential investor expressed interest in a particular investment, Madoff would tell them it wasn't available at that moment, creating an illusion of exclusivity. He knew that people crave exclusivity; everyone wants something not easily accessible, almost like a status symbol.

By the late 1990s and early 2000s, people were lining up to join, unaware they were part of a scam. Essentially, Madoff was just moving money from Peter to pay Paul, as the saying goes. The fraud grew so massive that Madoff maintained a bank account holding billions.

His luxurious lifestyle reflected that wealth, with luxury homes and yachts. He managed to keep the scam going for decades until the 2008 financial crisis hit. This global crisis triggered widespread fund withdrawals, and because many investors had already pulled money out before, the firm couldn't meet the huge redemption demands. This set off a huge investigation that led to Madoff's arrest.

Now, to revisit the earlier question of why Bernie Madoff did it—the answer, I believe, is that he got away with it for so long because he understood the golden rule: "He who has the gold makes the rules." This old cynical saying implies that those with wealth and power have the right to set the conditions and make the decisions. It essentially means that money equals influence, and those who possess money hold the greatest sway within a society or organization. The downfall of Bernie Madoff aligns with the common perception of liquidity —that is, how quickly and easily an asset can be turned into cash without losing much value.

While we're not all criminals, cash is universally seen by individuals, businesses, and governments as the ultimate tool of control. For example, imagine you're just starting out and lack a credit history but want to get a loan. The bank knows you have no credit record but is willing to take a chance because you have cash in the bank that can serve as collateral. They approve your loan, overlooking your credit profile because you're considered liquid. Do you see what happened? Your cash was used as leverage to secure the loan because cash will always be king. Believe it or not, many financial institutions will lend money based on the cash you have on hand.

The same principle applies to someone heading to a club who wants VIP treatment. They might buy out the bar, reserve a special section away from the crowd, and leave generous cash tips for the staff. The club manager would likely roll out the red carpet for that customer.

Having ready access to hard cash opens doors to many opportunities—opportunities that most people will never experience. Cash isn't only useful for splurging; it can help during emergencies that might be otherwise disastrous. It's also advantageous in business. Today, for example, if you want to own a McDonald's franchise, you need at least $500,000 in liquid assets for the corporation to consider you seriously. In essence, having cash allows you to create opportunities on your own terms because everyone understands that whoever controls the money sets the rules.

Credit, meanwhile, has a different nature.

Like cash, credit can create opportunities if used wisely. Credit is used to invest in businesses, purchase homes, or finance vehicles, but unlike cash—which is earned and owned—credit is lent to you temporarily on the promise you'll repay it based on your creditworthiness. When you pay with cash, the transaction ends immediately. Paying with credit, however, may feel like the transaction is complete, but it technically isn't until the debt is fully paid. This is where issues arise if you're not careful about paying off your debts.

Just to clarify, I am not a financial advisor or expert, nor am I offering specific financial advice. I'm simply sharing my past experiences and insights on how I've come to understand this subject. Without access to credit, buying certain essentials can be very difficult. Whether you like credit or not, we can all agree that life without it can be challenging.

Here are some tips on how to build or rebuild credit:

1. If you've never had credit but want to start building some, a good first step is to ask a close friend or family member you trust to add you as an authorized user on one of their credit accounts. This can be highly effective, provided that person has a good credit history with well-established accounts in good standing. The benefit is that if they have a solid credit profile built over time, you inherit that positive history as if it were your own, even if you have little

or nothing on your own credit record. You can go from having no credit to reaching a 700 credit score in as little as 3-6 months on one of your personal credit profiles.

This method is also effective for those looking to rebuild their credit.

2. Start by contacting the financial institution where you have an account and ask if they offer a secured credit card. Secured cards differ from traditional, or unsecured, credit cards, which don't require collateral. When applying for an unsecured card, you might need to provide proof of employment and income. In contrast, a secured credit card application will definitely require a cash deposit upfront. This deposit becomes your credit limit if approved. So, if you don't have a strong profile or any credit history for an unsecured card, a secured card is a good

alternative. Generally, if you have no credit or poor credit, you'll be seen as high risk, which means if you can't repay your debt, the deposit you made will be used to cover what you owe. Remember, the main reason for choosing a secured card is to build a good credit profile so you can eventually qualify for an unsecured card.

3. Another option is to apply for a credit builder loan, which works differently from a traditional loan. The lender sets up an account where you make fixed monthly payments to them. The full loan amount is held in this secured account until you finish the term. Once you make your last payment, you gain access to the money you've paid. I like this approach because it offers two benefits: making regular payments builds a strong payment history, which makes up about 35% of your credit score, and it also helps you save money

by depositing it in a kind of savings account.

Saving money while building credit should be an obvious win for anyone starting this journey. Be sure never to miss a payment, because just like traditional loans, a credit builder loan will report late payments, which can hurt your score.

4. To quickly boost your credit, regularly check your credit reports and dispute any errors, pay off all credit cards in full each month to avoid interest charges, and maintain a good mix of accounts on your profile. Lenders prefer to see both installment loans and revolving accounts. Lastly, and importantly, try to keep your credit utilization below 30%. For example, if your credit card limit is $1,000, avoid spending more than $300 before the statement date, as higher usage can negatively affect your score.

There are many ways to build and maintain a healthy credit profile; I could write a whole book just on this topic alone to cover everything. My aim isn't to overwhelm you with details but to provide enough information to spark your interest and encourage action.

These are some of the steps I took during my credit-building journey, so I know that if you put them into practice, they will work just as well for you.

CHAPTER HIGHLIGHTS

1. Liquidity offers stability.

2. Building wealth is impossible without access to credit.

3. Those who possess and control the cash make the rules.

7.

CHANNELING
EMOTIONS

"YOUR DISPOSITION IS
SHAPED BY HOW YOU
RESPOND TO
EVERY SITUATION"

Have you ever stopped to think about why humans are considered the most intelligent species on Earth? Some historians might offer a scientific rationale for our ongoing evolution into beings of advanced intellect. They could mention factors like our large brain size, the development of language, the ability to pass down culture and knowledge, among many others, which is undoubtedly true. However, in my view, there is one fundamental reason that outweighs all the others for why humans continue to dominate this planet: the power of the subconscious mind, which is closely connected to emotion. I explore the subconscious mind in detail in chapter 5. In this chapter, I want to focus on the idea of emotional intelligence.

Every thought we have sends out a signal, and every emotion we carry forms a pattern.

Our money habits closely reflect our emotions. Emotional intelligence is the ability to manage emotions effectively and efficiently. Once we recognize our emotions, we can begin to control them and even affect the emotions of those around us. How we perceive our emotions can make us either reactive or proactive. Being less reactive and more proactive in controlling your emotions is a clear sign of self-awareness. Learning to use your emotions to guide your thinking, rather than letting emotions drive your thoughts, benefits your environment and gives you the power to influence the world around you. Mastering this skill aids in social awareness, self-management, relationship management, and managing money.

Emotions have a strong connection with money. Every financial situation we've faced has triggered intense feelings, shaping how we handle our finances. This often results in financial choices motivated by feelings rather than logic. Stress about money can cause anxiety and depression, sometimes leading to a lack of drive to manage finances and even impulsive behaviors like overspending for a temporary sense of pleasure. It may also cause sleep problems, social withdrawal, and difficulty affording basic needs.

Financial stress not only affects emotions but also impacts mental health. So, how do emotions influence financial decisions? Most people make financial choices based on emotions more than logic, which can have both positive and negative effects.

Let's examine some emotions that influence these decisions:

FEAR AND ANXIETY

These emotions can encourage cautious spending and foster a habit of saving. They can also motivate you to buy life insurance or consult a financial advisor for long-term investments. However, fear and anxiety can also cause decision paralysis, leading you to avoid important actions like planning for retirement. Another downside could be withdrawing money from stocks or investment partnerships during economic downturns out of panic.

JOY AND HAPPINESS

These feelings bring optimism and encourage proactive financial planning. Joy and happiness often lead to positive outcomes through increased motivation and discipline. On the flip side, they can prompt impulsive spending for celebrations, such as splurging on an expensive dinner or upgrading your lifestyle after a promotion. They can also lead to spending beyond your means, like maxing out credit cards on wants rather than needs, or making large purchases without budgeting— such as booking an overseas vacation on credit and planning to cover it with future paychecks.

SADNESS AND BOREDOM

On a brighter side, these feelings can motivate you to seek support from family and experts to recognize and change unhelpful habits. This approach aids in breaking bad money habits and encourages the formation of positive financial behaviors. On the downside, sadness and boredom may lead to impulsive retail therapy, making purchases as a short- term escape. For example, after a breakup, you might resort to a spending spree to help distract yourself from the pain. Additionally, these emotions can decrease motivation for long-term financial planning and cause you to avoid important money-related tasks.

GREED AND ENVY

Greed and envy often carry negative stereotypes, but when it comes to money, they aren't always bad. In fact, a sense of greed and envy can fuel ambition and career growth. You might be drawn to competitive fields like insurance or sales management, where many people vie for a limited number of positions. This competition can generate a positive drive fueled by these emotions. However, greed and envy can also have harmful effects, such as taking risky, uncalculated chances. For instance, gambling or accumulating unnecessary debt are common pitfalls. Worse yet is ignoring the risks involved in investments, overlooking potential downsides in pursuit of gains.

SHAME AND GUILT

These emotions often lead to more careful spending and encourage saving habits that prevent repeating past errors. For example, someone who has damaged their credit and even filed for bankruptcy often gets a fresh start but is motivated by the desire to avoid the experience again. This creates a mindset geared toward making smarter, more informed financial choices through gained wisdom.

However, shame and guilt can also cause secretive spending away from family and friends, reluctance to seek financial advice, and most importantly, ignoring money problems until they become serious.

A helpful way to manage money more mindfully is to shift from emotional spending to a thoughtful, rational approach. Increase your self-awareness by monitoring your mood when it comes to spending. Always pause before making significant financial decisions, even if just for a few days. Don't hesitate to seek professional advice, and practice self- forgiveness.

Lastly, establish a realistic budget and keep a close watch on your cash flow. Track your income and expenses carefully. Emotions play a vital role in the human experience and have inspired many of the world's greatest cultural and scientific achievements.

Understanding how emotions affect your thoughts and behaviors can better equip you to make financially sound decisions anchored in emotional balance.

CHAPTER HIGHLIGHTS

1. Let your emotions guide your thinking rather than letting them control it.

2. The stoic always comes out on top.

3. Make a habit of practicing emotional intelligence every day.

8.
THE
ULTIMATE
SACRIFICE

"THE MOST CHALLENGING TASKS FREQUENTLY YIELD THE MOST SIGNIFICANT RESULTS"

The late, legendary Nipsey Hussle will always be remembered as one of the most influential musicians of his generation. Nipsey wasn't just a distinctive and innovative artist; he was also a shrewd businessman. He sparked a lot of debate when he dropped a mixtape called Crenshaw in 2013. Priced at a staggering $100, it included a concert experience for its first buyers—a move unheard of in the music world, drawing criticism from many within the hip-hop community. Despite that, Nipsey's marketing brilliance shone through as he sold over 1,000 copies of Crenshaw, establishing his savvy in both marketing and business.

Nipsey Hussle launched several other ventures that turned out to be huge wins. In 2017, he opened The Marathon Clothing store in the neighborhood where he grew up, which eventually led to a partnership with the internationally renowned sports brand Puma. The store featured a clever setup where customers could access exclusive content through QR codes attached to the merchandise, enhancing the overall experience. Another of his projects was Vector 90, a co-working space he co-founded aimed at helping underprivileged entrepreneurs who needed office space to get their startups off the ground. Nipsey also owned a restaurant, a phone store, a record label, and some real estate, showcasing his skill in diversifying across various sectors.

Every success story has its share of setbacks. Before Nipsey found success in music, he was deeply involved in street culture. There was a time when he had to hustle illegally, which led to run-ins with the law—a common tale among entertainers who rise from poverty to wealth. So, how does a kid from a tough neighborhood, surrounded by crime, manage to break free and become one of the most successful figures in a competitive industry? The answer lies largely in sacrifice.

Nipsey understood early that true success demands a price. But this price isn't about blood oaths or selling your soul, as some narrow-minded people might think. Instead, it's a more subtle exchange—giving up something good, or what seems good, for something better. For instance, Nipsey was making quick cash on the streets, but once he chose to focus on his music career, he had to stop hustling. To him, it felt like a step backward. He was used to raking in fast thousands daily on the streets, so shifting to music, where he initially made little money, felt like a financial setback.

People who reach the top of their fields do so through sacrifice: giving up the things they love temporarily and doing what others won't. When it comes to wealth, the rich don't deny themselves pleasures—they just delay them.

Many believe life is about comfort, but the truth is that anything worth pursuing brings some discomfort. Instead of spending money immediately on material things that lose value, financially wise individuals reinvest that money into assets that generate passive income, letting those assets cover their expenses.

For every liability you want to buy, there should be a plan for an asset to pay for it. I admit, this is a tough principle to live by. Today's world is obsessed with instant gratification. Most of us aren't willing to endure the short-term pain of delaying purchases for long-term gain.

Feeling uneasy today paves the way to becoming unstoppable tomorrow. This is a principle Warren Buffett follows closely.

Known as one of the greatest investors ever, Buffett currently leads Berkshire Hathaway as its chairman and CEO. Forbes estimates his net worth at around $160 billion, ranking him as the fifth richest person globally. Clearly, there's much we can learn from his approach. I remember being captivated by Buffett's method for evaluating stocks. It involves reading 500 pages daily, covering a range of materials such as books, newspapers, and financial reports from major companies. He dedicates 80% of his time to reading. Buffett believes that absorbing 500 pages of knowledge each day works like compounding interest in investing. Just as your money grows with compound interest over time, so does your understanding through consistent reading.

To become the best investor, Buffett is willing to do what most of us aren't.

The famous 10,000-hour rule has been around for some time, suggesting that expert-level skill requires at least 10,000 hours of practice. While some argue that natural talent also plays a part, time and effort remain crucial. One key lesson from both Warren Buffett and Nipsey Hussle is that time should be managed like money. Viewed this way, time is the only form of currency you can never reclaim. Mastering time management is a skill in itself. There are 168 hours in a week, and I challenge anyone to track how they spend each hour. You'll likely find much of it wasted on things that add no real value. This idle time can instead be invested in activities that nourish you and help you grow into a better version of yourself.

Making sacrifices to improve your life means trading short-term desires for what you truly need most, which often involves discomfort. When you commit to a goal, expect criticism from friends, family, and the world. The key is to ignore the noise and distractions by staying focused and following your plan. In the quest for success, you must be willing to be selfish before you can be selfless. Though it may sound harsh, this truth carries weight and demands a strong mindset.

Sacrificing moments with loved ones is tough and can breed resentment, but it is a challenge you must bear if you're serious about reaching your goals. Only you will truly understand what it takes to perform at your best, and often it's difficult to communicate that to others.

CHAPTER HIGHLIGHTS

1. Starting over shouldn't be perceived in the negative.

2. Tough choices involve prioritizing your needs instead of your desires.

3. In order to be selfless you must first become selfish.

9.
BUSINESS
AND
INVESTING

"THERE'S NO NEED TO
CREATE SOMETHING
ENTIRELY NEW;
SIMPLY ADJUST WHAT
EXISTS AND IMPROVE IT"

Ray Kroc is remembered as one of the most determined businessmen in modern history. Some would argue he combined the brilliance of Henry Ford with the work ethic of ten men. If you haven't heard of Ray Kroc, there's a 99.9% chance you've encountered the restaurant he built. The building that seems to stand on every major road in America, marked by those iconic Golden Arches, is none other than McDonald's. Although Ray didn't create the original McDonald's concept, he played a crucial role in its national and global growth.

Today, McDonald's is the largest restaurant chain in the U.S. by revenue and sales. It boasts over 41,000 locations worldwide in more than 100 countries, generates over $25 billion in annual sales, and feeds 1% of the world's population every day. Another interesting fact: McDonald's is the world's largest toy distributor because of its Happy Meals for kids. How did one man take a company and make it so widespread? One word—persistence. A famous quote inspired by the 30th U.S. President Calvin Coolidge goes:

Persistence, nothing in the world can take the place of persistence. Talent won't; nothing is more common than unsuccessful men with talent. Genius won't; unrewarded genius is practically a cliché. Education won't; the world is full of educated fools. Persistence and determination alone are all powerful. Show that you don't have to be defeated by anything, and that you can have peace of mind, improved health, and a never ceasing flow of energy; if you attempt each and everyday to achieve these things—the results will make themselves obvious to you. While it may sound like a magical notion, it is in you to create your own future. The greatest discovery of my generation is that human beings can alter their lives by altering their attitude of mind, or as Ralph Waldo Emerson declared, a man is what he thinks about all day long.

This belief helped Ray Kroc transform McDonald's. Ray began as a milkshake machine salesman, traveling to restaurants and pitching why they needed his machines. This approach worked for a while, sustaining his lifestyle but not changing it. Then in 1954, Ray's life took a turning point when he met the McDonald brothers in San Bernardino, California, while trying to sell them milkshake machines. The McDonald's restaurant required eight machines, which caught Ray's attention.

He was impressed by their "Speedy Service System" and eventually convinced the brothers to let him become the franchising agent.

Despite years of growth, what seemed profitable for franchisees wasn't as profitable for Ray.

Though the business was expanding, he sought solutions amid many challenges.

Then he met Harry Sonneborn, a financial expert, who advised him to focus on real estate to boost profits. Sonneborn suggested that Kroc buy the land for the McDonald's franchises and lease it to the franchisees under their operating agreements. This proved to be the most profitable decision McDonald's ever made. With income from leasing land, the company was no longer solely dependent on restaurant sales. This real estate strategy fueled the company's growth to what it is today. Ask the average McDonald's customer what business they're in, and they'll say fast food, but in reality, their main business is real estate. This is why McDonald's remains the most profitable food chain in the U.S. and worldwide. What set McDonald's apart from its rivals was its distinctive system.

For a business to succeed, having a strong system is always essential. Besides creating an excellent system, there are seven additional parts to running a successful business.

THE 8 COMPONENTS TO A SUCCESSFUL BUSINESS:

MISSION

This is the core principle on which the business was established. Every company has a mission statement.

LEADERSHIP

These are the partners responsible for demonstrating integrity and offering direction for the organization.

TEAM

This includes all individuals involved, each taking on a specific role and concentrating fully on it.

CASH FLOW

This is what sustains the business. All partners should be well-acquainted with quarterly and yearly sales figures.

COMMUNICATIONS

Consistent reporting to one another, regardless of the situation.

SYSTEMS

Guarantees the organization is well-structured and organized to maintain efficiency.

LEGAL

Assembling and hiring the right legal team to ensure the organization complies with local and state regulations.

PRODUCT/SERVICE

Delivering the highest quality products or services to the community.

Building wealth takes more than just the income you earn from a job. Launching a business or investing in one are two of the smartest approaches. In the U.S., many top earners grow their wealth by investing in the stock market and owning real estate. I'm not here to give investment advice, but from my experience, one highly effective way to invest in the stock market is through an index fund like the S&P 500. The S&P 500 is a stock market index that tracks 500 of the largest, most widely owned U.S. companies, acting as a gauge for the overall health of the U.S. stock market. If you're someone who doesn't know how to pick individual stocks or lacks the skill to analyze financial statements like Warren Buffett, investing in an index fund is a great choice. Instead of betting on one single stock, you're investing in a group of companies, giving you a stake in all 500 at once. What's great about the S&P 500 is its history of delivering a long-term annual return of about 10% since 1957, making it a relatively low-risk investment. Of course, all investments come with risks, and it's up to you as the investor to weigh the pros and cons. History shows that those who consistently save and automate investments into the S&P 500 will almost certainly see returns, as long as they have patience. Investing in a company generally requires less effort than starting a business from scratch. But if you have patience, a solid plan, a strong work ethic, and a bit of luck, the payoff can be significant.

As I've explored social media and the internet, I've noticed many so-called gurus, coaches, and overnight success stories all competing to take your money with promises of quick riches. Be very cautious of such people. Anyone trying to sell you a get-rich-quick scheme is usually full of nonsense. Sure, some people invest and get lucky with huge gains, but that's rare. Starting or investing in a business demands a lot of time and learning.

You also need emotional intelligence, discipline, and an unyielding drive to succeed. This explains why 90% of businesses don't survive past three years. To truly succeed in business, you often have to fail a few times.

Those failures are how your character is shaped in entrepreneurship. The next time someone claims to be a successful businessperson selling you an online course, ask them how many times they have failed. It's easy to sell off what you've achieved on the surface, but the real way to connect with people is to share the struggles it took to get there.

Owning a business and investing isn't for everyone and shouldn't be forced. There's nothing wrong with living off a salary alone, but if you genuinely want to build wealth, investing is essential. If you don't know where to start, reach out to financial planners, advisors, and mentors. Just make sure you carefully vet anyone you seek advice from.

Saving money for a rainy day is wise, but learning how to invest that money to grow it is even better in the long run.

Here's something worth noting: we're all born with two identities — our individual self and our business self. Our individual self is assigned a Social Security number automatically, but our business self gets nothing by default. The Social

Security number symbolizes us as tax-paying citizens with an obligation to work.

In contrast, the EIN (Employer Identification Number) represents our business self. You get the EIN when you apply to start a business. Essentially, it's like a Social Security number for a business. Isn't it odd that a social security number is handed out without a second thought, yet an EIN is only provided when specifically requested? There's definitely a hidden reason behind this, which I'd love to share, though it might make me sound like just another conspiracy theorist. I'm bringing this up simply to stress that we all should activate our second identity, even if running a business isn't on your agenda, because an EIN is about much more than just business operations.

Getting one can open financial opportunities that seem unimaginable to most people and plays a crucial role in building wealth that lasts for generations.

CHAPTER HIGHLIGHTS

1. Making smart and patient investments builds wealth that lasts for generations.

2. Focus on producing value instead of only consuming it.

3. Steady cash flow from investments holds far greater importance than relying on one paycheck.

10.
TRANSFORMATION REQUIRES ISOLATION

"DISTRACTIONS WILL APPEAR, BUT THE ABILITY TO FOCUS ON WHAT'S IMPORTANT IS WHAT SEPARATES THOSE WHO SUCCEED FROM THOSE WHO DON'T"

Ras Tafari Makonnen, better known globally as Haile Selassie I, ruled as Emperor of Ethiopia from 1930 to 1974. He was widely regarded as a pivotal figure in modern Ethiopian history. Throughout his reign, Selassie aimed to modernize Ethiopia by implementing political and social reforms. As the nation's leader, he understood the enormous responsibility he carried. After all, Ethiopia is where the oldest human remains were discovered and is one of the only two countries in Africa never formally colonized by a European power, making it the continent's oldest independent state.

Between 1887 and 1889, a conflict erupted between Italy and Ethiopia due to Italy's colonial ambitions. This conflict, now known as the first

Italian-Ethiopian War, ended in a strategic victory for Ethiopia.

However, 46 years later, in 1935, a vengeful Italian invasion sparked the second Italo-Ethiopian War. This time, the Ethiopians were less fortunate. Under Selassie's leadership, they were defeated and faced Italian occupation. The Emperor was then forced into exile in the United Kingdom. During his exile, the temporarily displaced Emperor gained British support, along with backing from other nations, to launch a campaign to restore Ethiopia's sovereignty.

Over these five years in exile, Selassie formulated a plan to join the United Nations, hoping to secure aid to reclaim his country. This strategy was highly successful, allowing the Emperor to return home with full authority once again. After his return, Ethiopia grew stronger, solidifying Selassie's legacy as a great leader.

If there is one key lesson from Haile Selassie, it is this: in moments of uncertainty and loss, sometimes stepping away is necessary to rise again. I genuinely believe that if Selassie had wished to remain and die for his country during the Italian occupation, he would have done so. Instead, he chose exile with the goal of returning more powerful for his people, accepting temporary defeat. We can all learn from Selassie's example.

Life presents many obstacles and setbacks, and often pride prevents us from stepping back or removing ourselves from certain situations to start anew. This idea is similar to how we manage our finances. Sometimes, handling money can feel overwhelming—whether it's due to heavy debt, obligations to family, or negative peer influences. Whatever the cause, it's wise to pull back and evaluate your situation.

If you are overwhelmed by debt, a practical approach is to develop a strategy for paying it off. You might set a specific monthly payment goal or consider reaching out to a debt consolidation service. For some, bankruptcy might be the last option. Whatever path you choose, make sure the decision is yours alone. The last thing you need is someone else telling you what they think you should do. This is where isolating yourself can be beneficial.

In a world filled with distractions and noise, some alone time might be just what we need. There's a saying: you are the average of the five people you spend the most time with.

When you really think about it, it makes perfect sense. If your five closest friends have no interest in financial intelligence, you're unlikely to be far ahead. I've learned that with finances, it's not about making the choices you want but about making the choices that are necessary.

You may be reading this now, aware that someone in your close circle affects you negatively when it comes to money. You don't want to come across as the friend who thinks they're better or as a traitor, so you stay close to this person until you're both broke and drowning in debt. Let me be the first to tell you that it's okay to step back temporarily from someone you care about if their influence on you, especially financially, is harmful. They might hold a grudge now, but your future self will appreciate your choice.

Life has a curious way of drawing us into solitude. We might feel punished, but that's not the truth. The main reason the universe pulls us into isolation is to prepare us to clear away all distractions and confusion so that the only voice left is our own.

Rebuilding yourself alone is a difficult process; it's painful and lonely, yet necessary. In the quiet and stillness, something starts to awaken within you—a fierce desire and strength you never knew you had. Silence holds a strange power: it can make the strongest feel vulnerable and the loneliest feel unseen. But inside that silence lies the groundwork for your transformation. When all the noise disappears and the crowd fades away, there's no one left to impress or owe anything to. That's when you truly confront yourself, and that's where real growth begins.

Many of us won't admit that our fear of silence comes from facing our own truths. It's easier to stay busy scrolling through social media or spending time with people who add no real value just to avoid hearing our own thoughts. Isolation doesn't show up to harm you; it appears so you can heal.

Jay-Z is undoubtedly one of my all-time favorite rappers—I'd say he's in my top five. I've always admired everything he's done in business, from owning his record label to partnering with the NFL. So when I heard back in 2004 that he was leaving the record label he co-founded in the mid-1990s, I didn't understand and felt disappointed. It wasn't until later, as I gained wisdom and grew, that I realized why he parted ways with the label he helped build. Jay was focused on growth and becoming a better businessman. He saw that the people he started with had grown complacent and hit a ceiling. Instead of watching the ship he built sink due to stagnation, he removed himself from toxic influences and leveled up dramatically. He went on to create a new music empire and strike deals that boosted his net worth well beyond $1 billion.

Looking at Jay-Z's achievements today, I fully processed why he split from his old partners. Jay carved out a path for growth and saw that the people around him didn't share that vision. He knew that isolation was essential for elevation.

CHAPTER HIGHLIGHTS

1. Don't fear spending time by yourself.

2. You become who you are through the five people you surround yourself with most.

3. Being constantly available lowers your worth.

www.ingramcontent.com/pod-product-compliance
Lightning Source LLC
Chambersburg PA
CBHW071702210326
41597CB00017B/2294